Psalm 49 (48)

Motet for Solo-Voice, Mixed Chorus and Orchestra/Organ

SZABÓ-SIKLÓDI LÁSZLÓ-LEVENTE

Trafford PUBLISHING® www.trafford.com
North America & international
toll-free: 1 888 232 4444 (USA & Canada)
fax: 812 355 4082

In memoriam:
Jakab LÁSZLÓ
et
Bán Anna

Foreword

A psalm represents sung poetry of the religious literature. It is widely used in both Jewish and Christian rites, being taken from the Bible. The *Book of Psalms* consists of 150 psalms and it is attributed to King David, King Salomon, the Sons of Korah and Asaph. This Psalm is identified as the 49th and the 48th depending on the Hebrew, respective Greek numbering. Psalm 49(48), as generally noted, belongs to the second Book from the collection of psalms, and comprises in its title: its recipient and its writer: *For the choir director. A psalm of the sons of Korah.*

On the next pages, an English translation of the psalm is provided to help the performers find the biblical meaning and interpret appropriately the Latin text[1]. *The Holman Christian Standard Bible* and *The New World Translation*[2] are presented below in order to observe different nuances of the word usage. There is no affiliation with any particular religious organization expressed here. For alternative translations, it may be considered the Jewish English collection of the psalms, *Tehillim*[3], and the Catholic Public Domain Version[4] of the *Book of Psalms*.

Szabó-Siklódi László-Levente creates an impressive and inspiring choral work for one solo voice, mixed chorus and a grand orchestra using the Latin text. The score includes the organ transcription, so that the psalm can be performed either with a large apparatus in a concert venue, or in a church, on a two or more manual organ with pedal. The work is designed as a medieval motet, in which each voice is set on a different verse of the psalm. The distinct voice movements and the text converge into a kaleidoscopic significance. Although not the entire text of the psalm is used, the verses selected preserve the meaning, and the message of the biblical text, which become enhanced by its profound music.

---

1   Complete Latin text can be found: Psalm 49(48), Liber Psalmorum, Nova Vulgata: Vatican website, http://www.vatican.va/archive/bible/nova_vulgata/documents/nova-vulgata_vt_psalmorum_lt.html#PSALMUS%2049.

2   HCSB (Holman Christian Standard Bible), 2007, Nashville, Tennessee, pg. 498;
NWT (New World Translation) 2013, Online Bible: Psalm 49:1-20,
https://www.jw.org/en/publications/bible/nwt/books/psalms/49.

3   The Complete Jewish Bible: K'tuvim, Tehilim; Chapter 49:1-21, Online Bible
http://www.chabad.org/library/bible_cdo/aid/16270/jewish/Chapter-49.htm.

4   CPDV (Catholic Public Domain Version) 2009: Psalm 48:1-21 https://www.bible.com/search/bible?q=Psalm%2048&version_id=42.
All websites have been accessed on 09.03.2017.

The music represents the spiritual walk between the worlds and it is written in the memory of the author's grandparents, whose death was witnessed in 2001. The music suggests a summer feel waiting for the autumn. Symbolically, this pulls into the desire to find ripeness through death. Despite this desire, the conscious of death leads to a breakdown. The solo voice brings a recitative on a B flat pedal, which is enriched polyphonically by the mixed chorus and the orchestra. The solo is a meditation on wisdom of the ripeness. This part builds into a deconstructive climax evoking the fall of the waters or the dissolution of the persona, and the desire to rest. Death is stillness at the end of the decay process.

2017

Mihaela Buhaiciuc
Lecturer in Vocal Performance
Transilvania University, Brasov, Romania

Psalm 49[5]

1 Hear this, all you peoples; listen, all you inhabitants of the world,

2 both small and great, rich and poor together.

3 My mouth speaks wisdom; my heart's meditation brings understanding.

4 I turn my ear to a proverb; I explain my riddle with a lyre.

5 Why should I fear in times of trouble? The iniquity of my foes surrounds me.

6 They trust in their wealth and boast of their abundant riches.

7 Yet these cannot redeem a person or pay his ransom to God -

8 since the price of redeeming him is too costly, one should forever stop crying -

9 so that he may live forever and not see the Pit.

10 For one can see the wise men die; the foolish and the senseless also pass away. Then they leave their wealth to others.

11 Their graves are their eternal homes, their homes from generation to generation, though they have named estates after themselves.

12 But despite his assets, man will not last; he is like the animals that perish.

13 This is the way of those who are arrogant, and of their followers, who approve of their words.

14 Like sheep they are headed for Sheol; Death will shepherd them. The upright will rule over them in the morning, and their form will waste away in Sheol, far from their lofty abode.

15 But God will redeem my life from the power of Sheol, and He will take me.

16 Do not be afraid when a man gets rich, when the wealth of his house increases.

17 For when he dies, he will take nothing at all; his wealth will not follow him down.

18 Though he praises himself during his lifetime – and people praise you when you do well for yourself –

19 he will go to the generation of his fathers; they will never see the light.

20 A man with valuable possessions but without understanding is like the animals that perish.

---

5   Scripture quotation marked HCSB have been taken from the Holman Christian Standard Bible, Nashville, Tennessee, 2007, pg 498-499.

Psalm 49[6]

Hear this, all you peoples.
Pay attention, all you inhabitants of the world,
Both small and great,
Rich and poor alike.
My own mouth will speak wisdom,
And the meditation of my heart will show understanding.
I will pay attention to a proverb;
I will expound my riddle with the harp.
Why should I fear during times of trouble
When I am surrounded by the evil of those trying to overthrow me?
Those who are trusting in their wealth
And who boast about their great riches,
None of them can ever redeem a brother
Or give to God a ransom for him,
(The ransom price for their life is so precious
That it is always beyond their reach);
That he should live forever and not see the pit.
He sees that even wise people die;
The stupid and the unreasoning perish together,
And they must leave their wealth to others.
Their inner wish is that their houses will last forever,
Their tents to generation after generation.
They have named their estates after themselves.
But man, although honored, will not remain;
He is no better than the beasts that perish.
This is the way of the stupid ones
And of those who follow them, who take pleasure in their empty words. (*Selah*)
They are assigned like sheep to the Grave.
Death will shepherd them;
The upright will rule over them in the morning.
Every trace of them will fade away;
The Grave rather than a palace will be their home.
But God will redeem me from the power of the Grave,
For he will take hold of me. (*Selah*)

---

6   English translation according to the New World Translation (NWT), 2013, Online Bible: Psalm 49:1-20, accessed on 08.10.2017.
https://www.jw.org/en/publications/bible/nwt/books/psalms/49.

Do not be afraid because a man becomes rich,
Because the splendor of his house increases,
For when he dies he can take nothing with him;
His splendor will not go down with him.
For during his lifetime he congratulates himself.
(People praise you when you prosper.)
But he finally joins the generation of his forefathers.
They will never again see the light.
A man who does not understand this, although honored,
Is no better than the beasts that perish.

Psalmus 48

In memoriam Jakab László et Bán Anna

4

7

Psalmus 48

In memoriam Jakab László et Bán Anna

Meno mosso (♩ = 50)

18

19

21